THE OTHER SIDE OF A DICE

THOUGHTS ON LOVE, HOPE & THINGS IN BETWEEN THEM!

HET PATEL

Made with ♥ on the Notion Press Platform
www.notionpress.com

TO,

MUMMY & PAPPA

FOR EACH & EVERYTHING!

Contents

Acknowledgements *ix*
1. Chapter 1 1
2. Chapter 2 2
3. Chapter 3 3
4. Chapter 4 4
5. Chapter 5 5
6. Chapter 6 6
7. Chapter 7 7
8. Chapter 8 8
9. Chapter 9 9
10. Chapter 10 10
11. Chapter 11 11
12. Chapter 12 12
13. Chapter 13 13
14. Chapter 14 15
15. Chapter 15 16
16. Chapter 16 18
17. Chapter 17 19
18. Chapter 18 20
19. Chapter 19 22
20. Chapter 20 24
21. Chapter 21 25
22. Chapter 22 26
23. Chapter 23 27
24. Chapter 24 28
25. Chapter 25 29

Contents

26. Chapter 26 31
27. Chapter 27 32
28. Chapter 28 34
29. Chapter 29 35
30. Chapter 30 36
31. Chapter 31 37
32. Chapter 32 38
33. Chapter 33 39
34. Chapter 34 40
35. Chapter 35 41
36. Chapter 36 42
37. Chapter 37 43
38. Chapter 38 44
39. Chapter 39 45
40. Chapter 40 47
41. Chapter 41 48
42. Chapter 42 49
43. Chapter 43 50
44. Chapter 44 51
45. Chapter 45 52
46. Chapter 46 53
47. Chapter 47 54
48. Chapter 48 55
49. Chapter 49 57
50. Chapter 50 58
51. Chapter 51 60

Contents

52. Chapter 52 61
53. Chapter 53 63
54. Chapter 54 64
55. Chapter 55 66
56. Chapter 56 67
57. Chapter 57 68
58. Chapter 58 69
59. Chapter 59 71
60. Chapter 60 72
61. Chapter 61 74
62. Chapter 62 75
63. Chapter 63 77
64. Chapter 64 78
65. Chapter 65 80
66. Chapter 66 81
67. Chapter 67 83
68. Chapter 68 85
69. Chapter 69 86
70. Chapter 70 88
71. Chapter 71 89
72. Chapter 72 90
73. Chapter 73 91
74. Chapter 74 92
75. Chapter 75 93
76. Chapter 76 95
77. Chapter 77 97

Contents

78. Chapter 78 98

79. Chapter 79 100

80. Chapter 80 102

81. Chapter 81 104

82 & To Be Continued! 107

Acknowledgements

Hilay, The Big Genius B. Thank you for always being there. What I love about you is your sense of humor. What I learned from you is to stay positive always. Also, This book wouldn't have been possible without your smartest advice to increase the vocabulary to express my true feelings into words.

I owe an enormous debt of gratitude to Ba for showering blessings from heaven. To My Family - Dada, for being the strong base of the family; Kaku & Kaki, for being lovely co-parents; Dhyan & Khanak, for keeping always energetic atmosphere in the house. Also, Thank you, my extended family, for your love & support.

I'm also immensely grateful to some great friends including Jeet, Raj, Pathik, Pranav, Nidhi & Many more. Thank you for always hear out stupid jokes & nonsense talks from the low-frequency-voice guy. Thank you for always being there.

I also want to acknowledge my college mates Harshad, Nikunj, Nihar, Ravi, Nirali, Dharmesh, Rajen, Rupesh, Payal & Many more - for making those four years memorable.

Thank you, All those friends and family members who undoubtedly helped in being the companions of my life journey till now.

Notionpress Publishing House, for shaping my words into this beautiful book.

Also, Thanks to the Corona warriors, you are making us proud by helping the world during this pandemic period. I hope, we will find the cure soon & see the world healthy and happy again.

CHAPTER ONE

A basic piece of development is change. Furthermore, this change happens in our sentiments, our inclinations, our preferences, and our side interests.

We're not continually going to feel the equivalent. Here and there, our inclinations, and our affection, will develop, though at different occasions, they will decrease or evaporate. And that is alright.

I understood that numerous leisure activities, companionships, and interests I had are gone. Previously, I'd battle and battle to remain the equivalent. In any case, presently, I understand this is representative of my development. I no longer need to battle to keep up whatever doesn't fuel my heart.

I will just battle for what I accept accommodates my objectives and my wants. I've changed a considerable lot of my inclinations, and I've lost numerous things en route. Be that as it may, I've picked up harmony, serenity, and more internal profundity.

This change once discomforted me. Presently, it represents my development. It keeps me longing for additional. Also, it's reinforced my confidence in what's to come. We won't generally feel the equivalent, and that is alright. That is development. That is change.

CHAPTER TWO

I have made, and keep on settling on, choices that many will never comprehend. That many laughs at and question. Also, I used to feel upset. Contemptible. I'd question why I wasn't "sufficient", or what I could do to gain acknowledgment.

I understood that the more I pursued outside approval, the more I was deep down discrediting myself. Disclosing to myself that others' decisions, and endorsement, made a difference more than my own.

That is the point at which I quit looking for an outward endorsement. Since there will consistently be individuals who object to my decisions, and who have reactions. They aren't me. They don't have my experience, nor do they have my cognizance, to realize why I'm on a specific excursion.

Also, I needn't bother with anybody to approve my choices. I will live for me and do what feels best. I will pick whatever activity, conviction framework, accomplice, and way of life is in arrangement with my most profound facts and my most profound self.

Along these lines, if any of you end up attempting to pick yourself, it's all right. It's ordinary. Keep in mind: it's your right. Not all will comprehend—and shouldn't.

We're all unique for social, strict, and individual reasons. In this way, we will pick them unexpectedly. Where we're picking self-satisfaction, we'll discover our direction.

CHAPTER THREE

I've been battling immensely of late. Managing numerous difficulties. Difficulties that are requesting my development and my rising, before they withdraw and award their shrewdness.

Furthermore, when I battle, I normally fall into a pit of uncertainty, apprehension, and vulnerability. At that point, the cycle proceeds, and I get down.

Yet, I advise myself that acomplishing an objective, giving up, and overcoming a test require some investment. They're not for the time being forms. Be that as it may, I'm utilized to moment satisfaction. I subliminally request prompt outcomes.

What's more, when I don't get them, I trust I'm either falling flat, or that something "isn't signified" for me. In any case, I'm showing myself tolerance, determination, and purposefulness. Figuring out how to be available, and to welcome the littler things.

Since postponements, and disappointments, don't represent dishonor and misalignment. They represent a requirement for development and refinement.

Along these lines, remind yourself, as I'm reminding myself, to show restraint, devoted, and decided. Use past triumphs as motivation.

I recall how I felt "off" when I previously began the exercise center, verse, and podcasting. It's not unexpected to be worried and dicey about new difficulties. Be that as it may, we can, and we will, learn and flourish.

CHAPTER FOUR

It took me some time to open up. Some time to have a sense of security enough to communicate my most profound certainties. I was adapted to accept that, on the off chance that I weren't a sure way, at that point I'd be a disappointment.

I'd invest so much energy hiding portions of me. Setting up veneers. Just commenting on what I thought would please individuals, as I kept on smothering my inward voice.

What's more, a piece of me was asking for enthusiastic freedom. For my spirit to allow my lips authorization to talk everything that would free me. Everything that would show me the way to realness.

So I began communicating. Begun seeking after what lined up with me, my realities, and my more profound reason. What's more, yes. I lost individuals en route. Yet, I additionally increased self esteem, and I picked up people who genuinely acknowledge me as I am.

Also, that is what I'm deserving of. I'm deserving of the individuals who respond the affection, the acknowledgment, and the glow that I award. I will not acknowledge anything less, or to be somebody else.

Also, that applies to every one of you. You shouldn't shroud what your identity is. You should grasp yourself. You're commendable. Furthermore, any individual who can't acknowledge you, doesn't merit your enormity.

CHAPTER FIVE

We as a whole experience focuses where we feel caught and alone. Where we feel like each entryway is shutting, and we'll never be cheerful.

In any case, we can leave. From the terrible relationship, the pestering activity, and the undesirable groups of friends. We should tune in to our sentiments. We should respect acts that offer freedom. Like leaving.

At the point when we leave, we're not stopping. We're understanding that it's an ideal opportunity to change and end the section. It's an ideal opportunity to go where we discover profound arrangement and satisfaction.

That is the thing that I understood. I didn't have to remain in a similar relationship, a similar activity, and similar decisions. I could leave—and it was entirely satisfactory.

In any case, I dreaded the torment and different assessments. Notwithstanding, looking back, I'm thrilled that I pick what fit me. What freed me and set my heart free. We merit bliss. What's more, now and then, we should leave to make it.

CHAPTER SIX

A large number of us experience the ill effects of what I call the "self-belittling complex", where we accept that everything is our issue. That we could have said more. We could have accomplished more. We could have been "something more." And that at last, our deficiencies prompted our deserting and this torment.

Be that as it may, it's an ideal opportunity to relinquish such inconvenient stories. Honestly, there is consistently "more" we could have done—and that is on the grounds that we're blemished people, and knowing the past will consistently supply these acknowledge. All things considered, it has nothing to do with our shamefulness.

Now and then, things don't work out for some reasons—others' injuries, terrible planning, and disaster. Be that as it may, it doesn't mean we should bear the responsibility. That is illustrative of quelled injury—continually bearing fault since we were never enough in youth.

You are sufficient. What's more, the individuals who esteem you, will accomplish the work. They'll comprehend, and they'll stroll with you. Any individual who doesn't, isn't intended for you.

CHAPTER SEVEN

Previously, I disguised dismissal. I trusted it was my caring ways and my expressiveness that sent individuals running. I disgraced myself. Guaranteed I'd cover my most profound parts, and work to become who I thought love required me to be.

However, at that point, I understood that affection is another layer of virtue. Also, immaculateness requires credibility. We can't manufacture certified associations with bogus personalities. Nor would we be able to discover develop spaces that respect what our identity is.

I would not like to give up my ways. I needed to clutch my center. Onto the brilliant angles that characterized what my identity was. Along these lines, I let go of inappropriate people. The individuals who'd never get me.

What's more, as I mended, I understood that individuals weren't dismissing me. They were dismissing realness, genuine affection, and validity. They were dismissing themselves. Individuals are just equipped for tolerating what they think they merit, and what they accept lines up with their earlier exercises.

What's more, whenever hurt, torment, and despair are their earlier exercises and their affiliations, at that point they won't have the option to acknowledge and value what's genuine. However, that isn't our deficiency. What's more, we shouldn't change what our identity is. How about we remain consistent with ourselves, so we can pull in what's intended for us.

CHAPTER EIGHT

I would think back and wonder to such an extent. What I could have said. What I could have done. How I could have been unique. What another person is doing, or in the event that they consider my life and my emotions.

I battled hard. In any case, at that point, I acculturated myself and recollected that considering is a piece of the human experience. We're interested in animals. We give it a second thought. We wonder. What's more, it's alright. We can permit ourselves to address it.

Be that as it may, we should recall that things end for reasons. What's more, however, we can't promptly comprehend, we will in the long run. We should figure out how to give up, with the goal that we may grasp what's coming. So we may proceed onward, and head toward what's in the divine arrangement.

I discovered that I might be disrupted and frustrated at a given time, yet that life changes and certainties uncover themselves gradually. I presently trust simultaneously, and I facilitate my way through. Every one of you can, as well.

CHAPTER NINE

We as a whole vibe awful and broken. However, we should recall that everything pass. Similarly as satisfaction and delight blur, in this way, as well, does torment and languishing.

You won't be broken until the end of time. You won't remain relationally stunted and apprehensive. You will mend. You will learn. You will turn into.

What's more, you will understand that you required each ounce of torment to become who you're intended to be. Since nothing incredible comes simple. We need to battle, and strain, to achieve what we need. On the off chance that it were so handily given to us, we'd never experience the procedure that refines us, and makes us what our identity is.

Along these lines, feel what you feel. Allow it to out. In any case, don't disregard your abilities. What's more, remember that emotions are impermanent. Goodness is directly around the bend. Change anticipates you. What's more, you can develop.

At last, you're not the only one. That is generally significant. We're all battling with something. What's more, we as a whole will make sense of it and win.

CHAPTER TEN

I understood that I was liable for my despondency. I attempted to organize my necessities, my needs, and my wants since I subliminally trusted I was contemptible.

I worked a hopeless activity, remained in inappropriate connections, and focused on exercises I would not like to do. It was negatively affecting me.

At the point when you live inauthentically, you diminish your own internal light. You keep yourself from drawing in what's intended for you, and from developing absolutely.

That is the point at which I understood that I expected to organize myself. I expected to pick the individuals, the exercises, and the existence that fit me. Since my joy matters. My decisions ought to mirror my most profound inward certainties.

Also, the equivalent applies to every one of you. That is no joke about needing change. For leaving. For choosing to live for you. It's your right. You have the right to liberate yourself, and to fuel your heart with decisions that fit.

CHAPTER ELEVEN

Our feelings are impressions of our instabilities and our injuries. That is the thing that I understood when I evaluated myself and my battles. I was envious. I begrudged others, and I in every case subliminally anticipated surrender.

I didn't have the foggiest idea what to do. I imagined that was only my temperament, and that I was destined to carry on with an envy tormented life. I was unable to control my dread of surrender. I misconstrued minor viewpoints as indications of another's looming takeoff.

In any case, I understood that desire was supported by my injuries and my instabilities. What's more, I additionally understood that I can recuperate these injuries. I can improve my confidence. I can effectively develop and shed these skins behind.

Along these lines, I began accomplishing the work. Started deprogramming old fashioned convictions. Occupied with exercises to help my confidence. Attempted to concentrate more on myself.

We don't need to keep these hindrances. We can fix them. We can supplant them with better musings and sentiments. It begins with recognizing them, and understanding that we can change.

I struggled with desire. Be that as it may, I've since figured out how to give up. To concentrate on myself. What's more, to recuperate, with the goal that more advantageous beliefs usurp more established ones.

CHAPTER TWELVE

Missing somebody doesn't mean you settled on an inappropriate choice. Nor does it imply that you're not recuperating.

It's OK to miss them. You shared valuable minutes. You became together. You took in a ton through each other. There is no disgrace in thinking back and valuing your previous joy and happiness.

Be delicate with yourself. Missing somebody is normal, and it's a piece of the lamenting procedure. This is the manner by which we train ourselves to give up, and how we figure out how to trust in what's to come.

Mending includes beating the torment of recalling. We as a whole experience it. Also, we as a whole get disappointed.

In any case, we understand that it works out. The farewells were vital, on the grounds that we wouldn't have developed without them.

CHAPTER THIRTEEN

I generally thought love was harming me—however it was my own examples. I was reproducing subliminal commonality by pursuing ladies who were disorderly, who wanted to make struggle, and who were inaccessible. Since that is the thing that I was utilized to from my youth.

I conveyed dread into my adulthood, accepting that affection would hurt me, and that it was contingent. Depended on my physical highlights and my capacity to be great. What's more, I'd abstain from getting excessively near individuals since I was burnt out on getting injured. Tired of feeling disgraceful and disappointed.

I would pursue ladies who were pugnacious and unstable. Ladies who made me continually battle for their great graces. Ladies who required somebody to continually fix them. Since that is the thing that I saw growing up.

What's more, this is the reason I needed to analyze myself internally. I was being informed that affection was wonderful, safe, and kind. However I was encountering the inverse.

I understood I wasn't pursuing adoration. I was pursuing a recognizable injury. A space that appeared to be conspicuous, and could fit in with my unfortunate propensities. That is the point at which I began accomplishing the work, and started evolving. Moving my examples. Reclassifying my convictions. Also, attempting to develop.

That can be applied to everybody. Love isn't the torment we have been familiar with. It's not the inaccessibility, the hurt, and the brokenness. It's the security, the dependability, and the glow we merit. What's more, in the event that we don't accomplish the work on ourselves, we'll battle to trust it.

CHAPTER FOURTEEN

I was accustomed to marking all dread based feelings as "awful." However that is not generally the situation. Here and there, I could be apprehensive, or wary, on the grounds that I'm new to an encounter or a circumstance.

Like a sound, adoring relationship. Like sound, common kinships. Like employments that need to offer me advancements. Like a stage where individuals are keen on what I need to state.

Since the entirety of this changed from my subliminal wellbeing zone: tumult and brokenness. A zone where I was just expected to think about others' feelings, as I relinquished my own. Where I never organized my standards and my qualities.

In this way, obviously, when something great went along—a superior opening for work, an extraordinary lady, or a decent stage to share my work—I dreaded it since it was unique. What's more, I didn't trust I was commendable. I despite everything battle with it now and again, as well.

We can't naturally term our feelings of dread and our questions as "terrible." They could be available in light of the fact that we're encountering subliminal deviations from our standards. We need to get accustomed to what's extraordinary. We need to take as much time as necessary. What's more, we need to accept that we're commendable.

I'm making little strides day by day. Building my confidence. Reaffirming my value. Filtering through my considerations and fixing old examples. It's alarming. My existence has never appeared to be so unsure. But on the other hand it's wonderful. Since it's never appeared to be so brilliant.

CHAPTER FIFTEEN

I tended to self-harm. I'd participate in initiating techniques: lashing out to increase one's consideration. Blowing up to little articulations, and driving individuals away. Disguising my internal realities, with the goal that none would ever get excessively close.

Be that as it may, I didn't understand these examples. I was unable to comprehend why love, and association, scared me. Why I couldn't normally subside into individual closeness and sharing insights regarding myself.

That is the point at which I chose to dive deep. I searched inside and rethought my subliminal relationship to adore, to association, and to closeness. I understood that my adolescence, which involved a temperamental relationship with parental figures, where I was damaged as often as possible, and compelled to smother my requirements, was showing in my adulthood.

I was driving individuals away. I was opposing closeness. I was removing love. Since affection, and association, were subliminally equivalent with youth hurt and torment. Also, I began accomplishing the work. Recuperating. Investigating. Opening myself, and giving weakness a possibility.

It feels extraordinary. However I'm despite everything taking a shot at to such an extent. I'm not completely recuperated. It will require some investment. In any case, I've understood much about myself, and I'm pleased with how far I've come. I am more cognizant, and I work to improve my subliminal affiliations, so I can sometime be simply the best man, supplier, and sweetheart for myself, my locale, my future spouse, and my future kids.

Our psyches constrain every one of us. Furthermore, it's dependent upon us to accomplish the work. It's an every day venture. We'll arrive.

CHAPTER SIXTEEN

I would frequently double-cross myself. Penance my requirements for other people. Swallow my words for their grins. Deny my validness, with the goal that I could fit into others' little standards. I wasn't living in my facts, nor was I communicating and battling for what I needed.

Also, that is the reason I was rotting inside. Why I was losing myself. This time, I needed to be acknowledged, however I wasn't tolerating myself. I disvalued my needs and my needs, continually organizing the sentiments of others. I disguised dismissal and felt separated.

Since when we don't communicate, or organize our qualities, we're subliminally disclosing to ourselves that we don't make a difference. Be that as it may, we do make a difference.

What's more, when I understood that, I ventured into my capacity. I don't conceal my sentiments any longer. Nor do I shroud my wants. I respect, and I feature, all pieces of myself. The great. The terrible. The dim. The turbulent. I grasp myself completely, while recognizing I have work to do.

What's more, any individual who can't acknowledge that, is allowed to leave my life. I will not endure halfway acknowledgment or half-love. I give completely acknowledgment and full love. In this way, I am deserving of accepting precisely what I give.

As are every one of you. Individuals will most likely be unable to respond. That is on them. In any case, you shouldn't endure indifference. You merit full acknowledgment, full love, and full space to develop. That acknowledgment will free you, and help you figure out what's intended for you.

CHAPTER SEVENTEEN

I've had my heart broken a couple of times. Be that as it may, I've likewise made my ownextremely upset. By fleeing based on what was acceptable. By looking for changed chances. By leaving too early, on the grounds that I felt "off." And by pursuing what I was never intended to get.

I carried on a huge part of my life trying to claim ignorance. It was such a great amount of simpler to nail the fault to other people. To blow up and revile the world.

However we are liable for our lives. Also, once in a while, we settle on choices that hurt our hearts. Choices that restrain our prosperity. I realize I've destroyed a lot of times. That is the reason I grasped responsibility, and started taking a gander at myself sympathetically.

Those missteps hurt. Those heartbreaks hurt. However, I'm thankful for each experience. For each second my heart was broken. Since it showed me how to confront my feelings of dread, how to rise, and how to synchronize myself with my feelings.

The force lives inside you. You can gain from your missteps. You can utilize them as a compass that guides you more profound into yourself. What's more, you would then be able to pick in an unexpected way, with the goal that you start obtaining the existence you want.

CHAPTER EIGHTEEN

I attempted to look after confidence. To have faith in the concealed. To put my trust in obscure circumstances, and to push ahead, despite the fact that I can't see the entire setting.

I incline toward substantial quality. Forces I can see, contact, taste, hear, and feel. It gives sureness—something I needed adolescence. Something that made the eccentricism that'd repulse me from adoration and from association.

I thought confidence—regardless of whether it be in religion, in convictions, and in different doctrines—was bogus and useless. I didn't think it dependably prompts truth—and perhaps it doesn't. In any case, numerous things don't dependably prompt truth. Nor would we be able to see with lucidity consistently. However we as a whole have confidence in something. In our capacity to deal with new conditions. In our conviction that another relationship will work. In our expectations that we can conquer already obscure battles.

Also, it takes a solid heart to have confidence. To have confidence in the concealed, and to stroll forward affectionately, and transparently, despite the fact that there is little proof to manage, and a major potential to get injured.

What's more, that is the reason I'm recognizing confidence, and recognizing the apparently mysterious powers that contrive to interconnect every one of us, and to take us to where we're intended to be. Everything starts with adoration. An adoration in us that urges us forward, and that reinforces us to seek after.

In case you're harmed, this is on the grounds that you're sufficiently able to accept, and to take risks in the concealed.

Furthermore, that is a force. That is a gift. Give yourself credit. What's more, presently, I'm available to confidence. I'm available to making the obscure strides and learning as I go. It's a lovely excursion.

CHAPTER NINETEEN

Society causes us to accept that we should have extraordinary purposes behind creation our choices. Your sweetheart/sweetheart is a not too bad individual? At that point you completely can't separate. Your activity offers better than average compensation and standard advantages? At that point you should remain. Another open door is excessively hazardous? At that point you can't do it.

These were a portion of the standards that were taught in me. Beliefs that tormented me and put me at chances with others. I struggled myself since, when I needed to set out on specific ways, I felt that I was "off-base" for doing it.

What's more, it finished as an almost here and there multi year relationship. I was disrupted. A solitary voice in me continued murmuring that I was intended to withdraw. That the time had come to seek after new roads. In any case, I stayed, expecting that this voice was beguiling and question ridden.

What's more, perhaps it was, to a limited degree. Be that as it may, I realized that there was a fact: I was in otherworldly misalignment. I expected to leave. Also, I did.

However it was hard, in light of the fact that she was an incredible individual. At the point when somebody is an "incredible" individual, at that point that implies we should make it work—as indicated by society.

In any case, I understood that it's more essential to follow your reality, and to do what frees you. To practice your wants, and to seek after what is in otherworldly arrangement. That is the point at which I left. Indeed, it made meextremely upset and broke my world. Be that as it may, it additionally set me free. It put me on the correct way, and it permitted me to respect my predetermination. I trust you'll do likewise.

CHAPTER TWENTY

I've been doing a ton of soul-looking of late. Crown has allowed me the chance to reconsider my past standpoints and perspectives.

What's more, it's hard. Confronting yourself, doubting your own stories, attempting to change, and mending will debilitate a great deal of your vitality. On occasion, I end up feeling miserable and vanquished. Having an inclination that it is highly unlikely out of this passage. That I may unremittingly feel lost and questionable.

In any case, I advise myself this is a piece of the excursion. Each extraordinary change is constantly gone before by trouble. That is the place we're tried, and where we're refined. I'm proceeding with this excursion, and I will appreciate the ride, as I develop, I learn, and I advance.

What's more, the equivalent is material to every one of you. Show restraint toward yourselves. Comprehend that it will be hard. You will be tested. Also, you will feel vanquished and purposeless on occasion. In any case, you will rise, you will learn, and you will turn into. Everything requires some investment.

CHAPTER TWENTY-ONE

I clung to my past. I conveyed lament and blame. I had a feeling that I didn't do what's needed, and that I didn't merit joy due to my slip-ups, and the way that I hurt others.

These convictions penetrated my life. Made me self-harm. To dismiss any great that came my direction, and to propagate patterns of brokenness and confusion.

In any case, I began accomplishing the work, and I understood that I was anticipating my past onto my present—and that is the reason everything was rehashing. Why my connections, and my endeavors would fall flat.

On the off chance that we don't work to mend, or to scrutinize our accounts, at that point we will battle to make the lives we want. We will be detainees to our antagonism.

Along these lines, I welcome every one of you to examine your most profound second thoughts. Consider what you realized, and how you developed. At that point, let them go. There is no compelling reason to reprimand yourself for past errors and bad behaviors.

Since we as a whole required our missteps to shape who we are today. It's an ideal opportunity to proceed onward, and to acknowledge that we are as yet deserving of affection and satisfaction. These acknowledge completely changed me, and I realize that they can do likewise for you!

CHAPTER TWENTY-TWO

At the point when I experienced dull occasions, it was difficult for me to see the positive qualities in myself. I attempted to accept that I was commendable, and that things could change.

Agony causes all of us to feel contemptible. It causes us to accept that we are never going to get what we're chasing, and that our negative sentiments include what our identity is.

In any case, it's critical to comprehend our agony. To sit with it, and tune in to everything it's letting us know, so we may become familiar with ourselves.

Torment is typical and inescapable. We won't be upbeat until the end of time. What's more, we won't be dismal, or tormented everlastingly, either. Everything blurs and we develop from the disturbance.

What's more, most basically: in any event, when we're feeling low, our integrity exists. All the affection, the glow, and the generosity we have are still there. They don't blur away. It's these characteristics that really make us what our identity is, and that merit our most elevated commendations.

Concentrate on the great. Concentrate on the characteristics you have that add to this world, and that help other people. Since they're generally there.

CHAPTER TWENTY-THREE

It's a wonderful blessing to feel profoundly. It requires colossal quality, significant passionate mindfulness, and a savage assurance.

Yet rather than applauding our extraordinary capacity to adore, we disgrace ourselves for getting injured. We feed our psyches bogus stories about affection's "pointlessness." And we keep ourselves from adoring once more, and conceivably constructing a suitable, productive relationship.

It's anything but a revile to feel. It's anything but an indication of shortcoming. It isn't continually going to be "the equivalent." The capacity to love will benefit you. It will push you toward more prominent statures, and it will keep on adding to your significance.

You have capacities that spare such a significant number of. That add to this present world's light. Also, it's an ideal opportunity to concentrate on the great, as opposed to disgracing yourself. Your adoration is a gift to such a large number of. You have the right to respect that.

CHAPTER TWENTY-FOUR

I'll always remember my last snapshot of accommodation a year ago. I was reeling. I was persevering through an impasse work, a terrible completion, and sentiments of uselessness.

Yet at the same time, a fire consumed in me. A fire convincing me to change, and to at long last start the change I realized I expected to encourage. I began taking a shot at myself. I got once more into the exercise center. Changed my eating routine. Understand more. Composed more. Altered a ton. Accomplished mental work to reinvent restricting convictions.

Also, I could never have done this, if my heart wasn't totally broken. In the event that my sentiments weren't wrecked.

Since nothing inspires us in excess of a messed up heart. However it is enabling. We can reconstruct our hearts, and ourselves, in the ways that best suit us. It prompts greater credibility and reason, which at that point lead to cherish.

Thus, in case you're down and out, this isn't the end. It's the start. It's a reintroduction to yourself, and a possibility for you to form who you need to be.

CHAPTER TWENTY-FIVE

For an amazing duration, numerous individuals, and numerous chances, left. I felt relinquished. Useless. Like there was some kind of problem with me, and that I was bound for solitariness and isolation. I disguised these flights as an arraignment of my character.

In any case, I understood that life, and the universe, are excessively immense for everything to be my flaw. Or on the other hand for me to continously disgrace, and deprecate, myself. Individuals leave since they have their own excursions. Openings blur since conditions change. We can't generally nail the fault to ourselves. That acknowledgment started my mending.

Regardless of who left, or what opportunity I missed, I despite everything benefited as much as possible from my circumstance, and wound up understanding that everything worked out. Had I would have landed certain positions, I would have wound up hopeless. Had I would have kept dating certain ladies, I could never have developed. Had I never gotten my heart broken, I could never have been constrained to change, and to start profound internal recuperating.

You are one individual in an immense, apparently unending, universe. With billions of individuals, minutes, and openings, close by you. Trust that this universe, and all it envelops in our reality, is working in support of yourself. That the connections are largely adjusting to shape a chain of enormity and satisfaction.

Since the universe, God, or whatever different powers we claim to, realize what we need. Furthermore, what we regard as a grievousness now, we will be grateful for some other time. Since it will be the explanation we have incredible fates.

CHAPTER TWENTY-SIX

Weakness was a genuine battle for me. I would not open up. I set up exteriors. Indicated bogus pictures and bogus grins. Shrouded my most profound parts. Kept discussions to surface level.

Also, I'd neglect to associate with others, without getting why. I trusted it was on the grounds that I was insufficient or deficient.

However, the fact of the matter was that nobody can associate profoundly to what's just surface level, or to what exactly isn't genuine. Individuals bond when they uncover their most genuine, most credible selves.

Since that is the thing that crushes the unreasonable idea of flawlessness. That is the thing that obliterates the obstructions between us, permitting our hearts to delight in each other's profundities.

We as a whole vibe like we need to disguise certain pieces of ourselves for adoration. It's what we were adapted to have confidence in youth. However, concealing what our identity is limits us from enjoying valid, profound associations.

Furthermore, that is the reason I changed. I grasp weakness. I show all of who I am. I recognize that it's alright to have defects, and that I am, and will consistently be, a constant show-stopper. Ever-evolving. Ever-developing. What's more, consistently deserving of living really and accepting affection. As are every one of you.

Be what your identity is. Show your every last bit of your rich profundity. That is the manner by which individuals interface. That is the way individuals make the most of what's genuine.

CHAPTER TWENTY-SEVEN

At the point when somebody leaves, or rejects our affection, we regularly confuse such activities as an attack against our value. We disclose to ourselves that, in the event that we were a greater amount of "this" or "that", at that point they'd remain and acknowledge our adoration. They'd respect what our identity is.

In any case, that is our instabilities, and our injuries, talking. Another's conduct is an impression of them. Your conduct is an impression of you. What's more, on the off chance that you appear, love hard, respect another, and do your part, at that point you are commendable.

However in the event that others can't acknowledge such love and respond, that is on them. Individuals frequently experience issues tolerating, and responding, love since they're inside injured. They have numerous injuries pulling them away from solid situations.

Furthermore, that has nothing to do with us. We can't control the pasts and the torments others are conveying. The past and the agonies which confine them from opening up, seeing their own worth, and tolerating love.

I was that individual. I opposed solid love. Great situations. Thoughtfulness and warmth. I was unable to perceive love as anything past the injury and the confusion I encountered. I needed to recuperate. I needed to burrow profoundly, question my own stories, and work to improve. It wasn't about the ladies. It was about me and my internal injuries.

Furthermore, the equivalent applies to every one of you. On the off chance that somebody has left and dismissed the extraordinary love you're offering, it isn't about you. It's about them and the work they've yet to do. Wish them the best. They need mending, and it is out of your control. You're doing what's needed. What's more, you are sufficient.

CHAPTER TWENTY-EIGHT

A significant number of us are excessively self-basic. We disgrace ourselves for feeling hurt. For being broken. For bemoaning misfortunes and disappointments.

In any case, we don't give ourselves acknowledgment for being sufficiently able to feel. Sufficiently able to adore without desires, and to give a valiant effort. It's time we rethink our psychological stories, and we see exactly how rousing, cherishing, and decided we are.

Life can be unpleasant. It includes a ton of hurt, injury, and challenges. Also, the most delightful viewpoint is human flexibility. The capacity, and the quality, to stay consistent with our character, regardless of how frequently we cushion and self-destruct.

Nothing represents quality better than one who will not give up their thoughtfulness and their caring approaches to their hurt, their annoyance, and their agony.

That is a demonstration of your quality. That is an outline of your value, and what you're made out of. Recognition yourself for your quality, your caring ways, and your tough heart. You merit it.

CHAPTER TWENTY-NINE

Ordinarily, when I was harmed or persevering through an incredible misfortune, I'd become mixed up in the torment. I'd revile the skies. I'd holler in isolation. Marvel why I needed to unendingly endure and pain.

In any case, it generally worked out. By one way or another, someway, everything would become all-good. An explanation would consistently show up, at some given time or another, and it'd explain my agony and saturate me with appreciation. I'd understand that, if not for a specific occasion, or a specific disaster, I wouldn't have encountered the essential realignment. I wouldn't have developed.

Also, that is the thing that I need every one of you to recollect. Regardless of what you're suffering, there is an explanation. There is a more noteworthy reason in this universe that is scheming for your development, your advancement, and your change. Cling to discover it.

It will cause separations, heartbreaks, and annihilating misfortunes. Be that as it may, it will likewise give new love, new chances, and another rendition of yourself and your life.

To get, we should be happy to give. Furthermore, once in a while, it requires giving up our previous lifestyles and our old expectations and dreams. Be that as it may, what shows up, is far superior than what leaves. It serves what your identity is, and who you need to turn into. Trust all the while. Also, believe that you will grin once more.

CHAPTER THIRTY

The greatest misunderstanding pervading our general public is that we should be immaculate to get love. That we can't be acknowledged, acknowledged, and delighted in for what our identity is, as we develop.

We accept that we should be impeccable. That we must be our best selves, before anybody can acknowledge us, and enjoy our inward profundities.

Be that as it may, this is unequivocally why we don't encounter sincere associations and wondrous minutes. Since we're too bustling covering ourselves, saying we're sufficiently bad, and staying away from chances to show who we genuinely are defenselessly, with the goal that we can bond, interface, and love.

Flawlessness isn't adorable. Since it doesn't exist. It's immaterial. It's simpler for individuals to connect themselves to your weaknesses, your blemishes, and your most genuine parts since they're genuine. They're unmistakable. What's more, they're relatable.

We discover bits of ourselves in crude humanness. In the pieces and edges of others that show likenesses to ourselves.

What's more, on the off chance that anybody expects us to be ideal for their adoration, they're not for us. They harbor unreasonable desires due to their injuries. That is on them. Not you. You're sufficient as you may be, and you can develop as you gain love. That is the excellence of being human. That is the magnificence of affection.

CHAPTER THIRTY-ONE

It's anything but difficult to lose all sense of direction in torment. To gaze at the messed up pieces, and to see our hurt, vanquished internal identity in its appearance. A zenith of strain and uncertain injury.

Since one deplorability, or one disappointment, isn't only one. Our brain makes an amalgamation of the entirety of our past agonies and stores it. At that point, we anticipate uncertainty, hurt, and dread onto our present.

Be that as it may, we're feeling the loss of a key exercise: torment is simply the ideal chance to reproduce. It offers us lucidity. We're at long last incited to search internally, to evaluate our most broken parts, and to recover who we need to be.

That was my story barely a year back. I was reeling from bidding farewell to somebody who had been a gigantic piece of my life, I was overweight, and I was uncertain of my future. I was anguish blasted. In any case, I wouldn't stop.

I permitted my troubles to refine me. To put their hands profound into my spirit, to retouch its pieces, and to reflect who I really am. I gathered exercises from everything, and utilized them to revamp. I started an excursion of escalated recuperating and recuperation. What's more, I was unable to be more appreciative.

Thus, perhaps you're in a similar circumstance. Perhaps you're harming, or you're uncertain. It's ordinary! We as a whole experience it. However, you can reveal the exercises, and use them to shape another life.

CHAPTER THIRTY-TWO

Individuals' behavior is an impression of them. They have their own injuries, troubles, and internal accounts to survive.

In any case, when we have our own instabilities and torments, we disguise their activities. We accept that it's our deficiency. I used to accept such things—I despite everything battle now and again. I advise myself that I am sufficient, in all the manners in which I've appeared.

Furthermore, we as a whole are. It's not our issue that individuals have injuries and torments. We can just help them. They may leave our lives. However, it doesn't characterize us. We keep on characterizing what our identity is, by how we carry on with our lives.

For whatever length of time that we realize we're appearing and doing our part, at that point we don't have anything to stress over. We can hold our heads high.

We should all desire each other the best, and advise ourselves that every individual is liable for their own mending and their own movement. Everything works out.

CHAPTER THIRTY-THREE

A solid association ought to be protected. It ought to be warm, welcoming, and sweeping. It will welcome you to step into your capacity, your realities, and your mending.

Be that as it may, a significant number of us are accustomed to hiding our most profound, darkest parts for adoration. Possibly we were harmed when we had a go at opening up. Possibly somebody disgraced us and revealed to us who we ought to be, and how we should act.

All things considered, we will never assemble the correct associations, with the perfect individuals, in case we're setting up veneers. In case we're retaining who genuinely are.

Any individual who doesn't acknowledge you isn't intended for you. It's that basic. Also, it doesn't imply that you're dishonorable. It implies that the universe is adjusting you for something better. For the spots, the individuals, and the open doors that will completely luxuriate in your inward lights.

No all the more imagining. No additionally covering up. How about we grasp validness—and that incorporates the most profound fissure, and the closest to home breaks, of our center.

CHAPTER THIRTY-FOUR

None of us need to lose somebody. Nor would we like to give up. It damages to say goodbye to somebody we've invested huge energy with. Somebody who saw the absolute most profound openings of our souls, and who held a sheltered space.

In any case, there comes a moment that clutching somebody implies relinquishing ourselves. Relinquishing our hearts. Neglecting to perceive what our identity is. Furthermore, that is not loved. That is codependency. That is harmful. That is injury holding.

We're worth more than that. We're worth joy, graciousness, and responded love. Be that as it may, on the off chance that we fasten ourselves to circumstances, and to individuals, who aren't coordinating what we're giving, at that point we'll carry on with lives of hardship and wretchedness.

Giving up, and beginning once again, is startling. None of us appreciate wandering into the obscure. We relish wellbeing, security, and consistency. Be that as it may, the obscure can be wonderful. It very well may be promising. Brimming with trust. Of new chances. Of individuals, and minutes, that will respect what our identity is.

Barely one year prior, I needed to give up. Of a darling. Of work condition. Of old bits of myself. Be that as it may, I have been acquainted with the profound, mental, and individual arrangements. I am a greater amount of myself. Also, giving up drove the way.

CHAPTER THIRTY-FIVE

I used to disgrace myself for adoring. For feeling profound. I'd regret the torment in my heart upon heartbreaks. Revile me for contributing more than the other. I permitted my torment to eclipse the magnificence. The magnificence that I, with the entirety of my profundity, had the quality, the will, and the ability to adore hard, and to battle for what I had faith in.

What's more, that is the thing that I need every one of you to perceive. Recognize your torment. The exercises. The hurt. Yet additionally recognize your capacity to adore, and to show others the best pieces of themselves, as you respect, and feel, your own. Not all have the ability to love to such profundities. Not all can so readily, and transparently, give hopeless bits of themselves.

However, you can. Furthermore, you have. You have appeared in enormous manners—and your agony is a confirmation. Adoring another can hurt us.

Be that as it may, it is this affection in our heart that guides us to the ways that will offer satisfaction, bliss, and worth. That mends, that spares, and that recharges the world's expectation. Try not to be embarrassed about that. Try not to conceal it. Fuel that adoration, and permit it to lead you.

I no longer disgrace myself for adoring. I perceive, and respect, the profundity I have which helps every one of my interests. I'm pleased to use such affection and to guide it to the world's improvement and mending. There is such a great amount of magnificence in the manner we love and break, and love once more. I trust you discover it. At that point, you will acknowledge you aren't the issue. You're following your excursion.

CHAPTER THIRTY-SIX

I used to put a schedule on my mending. I imagined that I needed to accomplish a specific measure of development at a given time. That I ought to have been over a specific circumstances after a given time.

However, these musings were counterproductive. Since mending isn't direct. It's capricious. It's unstable. It includes an arduous procedure involving profound reflection, injury affirmation, and psychological reevaluating. Thus, when we don't have our ideal outcomes, we become disappointed and we start to condemn ourselves.

There is no plan for mending. Truly, we can urge ourselves to give up. To push ahead. To pardon. In any case, we can't surge the procedure, nor would we be able to coordinate others' directions.

Everybody is on their own excursion, experiencing various encounters. Conveying various injuries. Battling against various social, strict, cultural, and social burdens. In this way, we're all going to recuperate at different rates.

What's more, there's nothing amiss with that. It's our exertion that issues. Our exertion that will move us forward. That is the reason we should rise every day, regardless of what unfolds.

Honestly, I'm despite everything mending. From numerous torments and injuries. Yet, presently, I don't surge myself. I take it every day, and I learn as I go. I realize that I don't have all the appropriate responses. Nor am I a specialist. Everything following a course. The manner in which it's intended to. Reveal to yourself the equivalent.

CHAPTER THIRTY-SEVEN

We're all here hoping to develop ourselves. To mend. To accommodate. To conquer our previous agonies.

Furthermore, along with this undertaking, we are battling profoundly settled in designs. Examples we have clung to for quite a long time. To have a sense of security. To fit in. To endure and to have a place. In this way, it isn't unexpected to feel like we will never show signs of change. To battle and to fight. To backslide and return to old propensities and old schedules.

Be that as it may, we can change. Also, it will occur, step by step. Consistently, we will work on the old covering. Gradually, pieces will tumble off, until it totally falls away, and we're exposed, in our actual structure.

Uncertainty and battle are natural pieces of progress. We're conflicting with what we're utilized to. We're going to feel troubled and uncertain. Be that as it may, we can go ahead in any case. Since change and the quest for self aren't started just when we feel intrepid.

We start whole we're dreadful and far fetched. We start since we're worn out, and we have the right to be glad. We have the right to break old examples. Furthermore, we will.

Thus, when you're battling, and when negative self-talk emerges, recognize it. Realize that it's typical. What's more, recollect that you are not your old considerations and examples. You are encased in a suit of covering you never picked. Also, you will get through it. You will emanate as your most genuine self.

CHAPTER THIRTY-EIGHT

At the point when we have an unfortunate connection style, contained weaknesses, injuries, and agonies, we will disguise others' practices. We will accept that it is our shortcoming.

Be that as it may, individuals' conduct is an impression of them. It gives us how injured they are. It isn't characteristic of what we merit.

It's significant that we make that qualification. That we understand that we're the ones who characterize our own value. We're the ones who hold the ability to characterize our worth.

What's more, we're the ones who can understand that individuals hurt us since they, themselves, are harmed. They are in dull spots, where they can't comprehend, nor welcome, our light.

This isn't tolerating the conduct, either. It's changing the account, sympathizing, and giving up. Thus, I welcome every one of you to excuse the individuals who hurt you, and to release the hurt. It's an ideal opportunity to leave. To push ahead. Also, to understand that we are more prominent than the agony that has been dispensed upon us.

CHAPTER THIRTY-NINE

A large number of us characteristic enthusiastic articulation, and weakness, with shortcoming. We feel that in the event that we show our emotions, at that point others will misuse us.

We convey these unfortunate affiliations and wounds on account of past torment. We need to abstain from getting injured once more, and feeling somebody's joke with respect to our gentlest spots.

Be that as it may, weakness, and enthusiastic articulation, are extraordinary indications of solidarity. It takes a great deal of boldness to show your most genuine self, in its rawest, most open structure. With your blemishes, your uncertainties, and your questions.

However, this is the means by which we truly interface with others, since we pulverize the ridiculous desires, and the hallucination, of flawlessness. This is the means by which we see excellence in being human.

Truly, there are individuals out there who have harmed us. Who has caused us to feel as were we "powerless" and "trivial" due to our most genuine parts and our most profound emotions?

In any case, those are injured individuals themselves. Individuals who are caught in unfortunate belief systems that will torment them, and forestall them, from associating profoundly. They are anticipating their misshaped recognitions onto us, and it isn't our flaw.

Be your generally open, most genuine self. Grasp weakness. Grasp your emotions. Grasp every one of your parts, and show them to the individuals who matter. Since that is the manner by which you'll fabricate a profound bond, and that is the way you'll encounter enthusiastic satisfaction.

In the event that we proceed with enthusiastic restraint, we will make them satisfy predictions. Individuals will leave. We will neglect to associate. What's more, we will be harmed. In any case, it won't be any other person's issue. It will be our own flaw. Since we are permitting our apprehensions, and our previous torments, to confine us from being powerless and open—the very demonstrations that permit us to interface absolutely. How about we change that.

CHAPTER FORTY

We regularly center around the goal. Picking up somebody's adoration. Landing recruited for that position. Finishing a task.

In any case, we overlook that the goal is just a single part. The excursion is the greater part. It stirs our boldness when we venture out. It manufactures our character as we test our grit, and propel ourselves forward. It encourages our development as we experience new things and become more acquainted with ourselves more profound.

The result is fairly inconsequential, when compared with our development, our exercises, and our own refinement. It is the character we assemble that decides the course of our lives.

Perhaps you got your heart broken. Possibly you missed that activity. Perhaps you neglected to finish that venture. In any case, you despite everything took in a great deal through those excursions. You despite everything added pieces to your character.

Also, that is what matters. Those are the minutes that will extend your quality, your insight, and your understanding. That is the manner by which you'll develop. In this way, stop. Pause for a minute. Reflect. Regardless of whether you accomplished your ideal result is negligible. The genuine respect is part-taking in the excursion itself, and in being fearless enough to step forward.

What's more, your messed up heart, your bombed venture, and your lost open door are a demonstration of that. Give yourself acknowledgment for attempting. You're doing what's necessary. At any rate you have the mental fortitude to attempt, to adore, and to battle for what you have confidence in. That is the thing that characterizes you. Nothing else.

CHAPTER FORTY-ONE

You will never recuperate in case you're driving yourself to overlook individuals. To eradicate the recollections and the exercises. Mending isn't overlooking others or canceling sentiments. Mending is tolerating. Tolerating reality, the agony, and the brokenness.

What's more, recognition does unquestionably greater than it does awful. Recalling your previous encounters permits you to find out what's intended for you, and what isn't. It helps you to remember your preferences, your abhorrences, and what you can and can't endure. What your non-negotiables are .

Thus, on the off chance that you decide to eradicate your encounters and your emotions, you're denying yourself of utilizing the very pieces you have to build up a firm establishment for your future. A firm establishment that starts the trend for the correct love, the opportune individuals, and the correct adaptation of yourself.

Torment isn't your adversary. Torment is an update. It manages your sentiments and your contemplations. It conjoins your most profound parts. Furthermore, it permits you to turn out to be entirety. It gives you what you need, and how you can accomplish it.

Your previous encounters are your best resources. What's more, they will assist you with the development of a superior life. They fill in as an unassuming aide, making you starting with one move then onto the next. Remember them. Grasp them. Gain from them. Also, develop to accomplish the life and the affection you merit.

CHAPTER FORTY-TWO

I was consistently terrified of sincerely communicating. I expected that I'd be relinquished if I somehow happened to go to bat for my most profound convictions and emotions. I never understood my own value.

Basically, my inaction was denying me of minutes to build up my self-esteem and to free my life of individuals who didn't have a place in it. Individuals who wouldn't have acknowledged who I genuinely am.

It's a gigantic error to smother our affections for the association. The associations wind up being inauthentic and useless, in light of the fact that they're not set up with any genuine ties.

You reserve each privilege to be what your identity is and to share your most profound realities. To broadcast what sits in your heart. Furthermore, on the off chance that anybody leaves your life after, let them go. They were never implied for you. They're helping you out, on the grounds that your life will be better when you can welcome tolerating, warm individuals in. Individuals who won't judge you, yet who will try to comprehend.

Your capacity and your value are characterized by the manner in which you go to bat for yourself. Passionate articulation is a basic part. You will never feel fulfilled in case you're stifling your contemplations and your emotions. That is basically disclosing to yourself that your considerations and your emotions are negligible—when they're most certainly not. They mean the world. What's more, you have the right to communicate with them.

CHAPTER FORTY-THREE

We have to rethink the manner in which we see circumstances, and the stories we let ourselves know. That is the thing that has the effect. That is the thing that decides how we recuperate, and how we push ahead.

As yet feeling hurt over a lost sweetheart or a botched chance, doesn't make you "feeble." that negative perspective is self-deploring, and it'll keep you caught in hurt. Also, it keeps you from understanding your capacity and your blessings.

Since having the option to cherish profoundly, and to see profoundly into another spirit, is a blessing. It is power. You're despite everything harming in light of the fact that you took advantage of that force and you accepted. Very few can do that. Be that as it may, you do. You open yourself wonderfully and you permit your heart to meander unreservedly. To adore with its whole.

Also, that is the reason you despite everything hurt. Not on the grounds that you're powerless. But since you have extraordinary profundity and can cherish past what many can.

Not any more self-belittling. Not any more negative inward exchange. The manner in which we see things, and the accounts we let ourselves know, sway how we push ahead. Take the two situations I introduced previously. You can decide to consider yourself to be feeble for as yet feeling hurt (in spite of the fact that you're not), or you can decide to see that those emotions are a demonstration of your capacity and your brilliant heart.

The decision is yours. What's more, I trust you pick thoughtfulness and empathy. You merit it.

CHAPTER FORTY-FOUR

It's so natural to accept that we will never be upbeat again. That we will continuously battle and feel torment.

The psyche is acceptable at that. It replays old scenes and looks for inevitable outcomes to have a sense of security and to look after recognition. In any case, you can rework these accounts. You can address them and help yourself to remember all your most noteworthy victories.

You've generally beaten your tragedy. Also, you've generally figured out how to cherish once more. That is your most noteworthy force. Furthermore, you should never give up on cynicism. You should never give up. Since this world needs unadulterated love. The very love your heart conveys.

It's not unexpected to feel like we'll never cherish again, and that we will be trapped. We will be tormented for all time. Be that as it may, that isn't the situation. There is consistently an exit plan. Continuously an approach to recuperate and get renewed. Furthermore, it begins in our brains. In fixing and remodeling old fashioned stories, and helping our hearts to remember all they've survived.

It doesn't get simpler. Each time we love, we develop new profundities, and it's more to recuperate from. But on the other hand, it's more to develop with. More to gain from. Also, more to work with. Always remember that.

CHAPTER FORTY-FIVE

Huge numbers of us accept that we should remain the equivalent to fit in, to get love, and to keep up our own social request. Furthermore, I can't accuse us. We were adapted to accept that we should be a sure way and that we should altruism for the association.

Be that as it may, our necessities, our emotions, and our wants are unmistakably more significant than modest, distorted associations. Associations that are manufactured inauthentically, on the grounds that we're hesitant to be what our identity is. We can recover our distinction by finding our wants and needs, and afterward regarding them.

What's more, this includes leaving the individuals, the spots, and the conditions that aren't in arrangement with what our identity is. The very perspectives that smother our enthusiasm. That dry out our development procedure. That drives us to be somebody else.

You don't need to remain in that relationship. You don't need to continue working that activity. You don't need to remain in a similar group of friends. You reserve each option to seek after the affection, the kinships, and the open doors that guide your development and supplement your inward light.

CHAPTER FORTY-SIX

We don't give ourselves enough credit. As opposed to lauding our advancement, we lament our pasts. We scrutinize ourselves for our mix-ups and bad behaviors.

Be that as it may, this is what it slips we's mind: it's simple now after we've reflected, we've learned, and we've developed, to lament. To mourn previous decisions. Also, to ponder unreasonably.

However, what your identity is currently isn't who you were at that point. You've changed. You've advanced. You see the world in an unexpected way. What's more, you are who you are a direct result of your past and your errors. They have shaped this person. Lit up the way and demonstrated you the way.

Furthermore, we owe our previous selves for all that we are today. We could never have bloomed without the pasts that have watered us.

It's an ideal opportunity to excuse ourselves and to give up. We required our pasts to be who we are today. What's more, there will never be any disgrace in development. Nor is learning as we go.

Measure your advancement. Measure your development. Measure your acknowledge. Respect yourself and have pride in your excursion. You merit it. We're all defective, and we're on this excursion together.

CHAPTER FORTY-SEVEN

We invest quite a bit of our energy ruminating on past darlings. Ruminating on what we lost and on their expected return.

In any case, as we ruminate, we neglect to empty our vitality into ourselves. Into our objectives. Into the existence that we can assemble. Since that issue more than anything. There is no more prominent obligation than the development of your best self. At the point when you're at your best, you can help out you, and for your separate society.

Also, I have faith in something: the individuals who genuinely love you will consistently discover their way back to you. Regardless of the time. Regardless of the separation. Regardless of the troubles. It will occur. The universe, god, or anything you desire to term it will scheme for it.

In this way, don't stick around. Put resources into yourself. Live for you. At the point when you are your best self, you draw in more prominent chances and more noteworthy vitality. Put stock in that. What's more, accept that you will accomplish whatever is intended for you.

CHAPTER FORTY-EIGHT

I was unable to acknowledge my errors. I upbraided myself. Thought I was the most noticeably awful individual. That I wasn't deserving of affection and of empathy since I settled on decisions that hurt others.

I neglected to understand that slip-ups display our humankind. We're defective. We're going to wreck and hurt others. We will settle on decisions that will break different hearts. What's more, we'll feel terrible about it.

In any case, we should recall that hurt is unavoidable, and one's opportunity and option to seek after their own excursion far overrides everything else. Harming others doesn't make you to a lesser extent an individual. It's a characteristic piece of the procedure. The key is to gain from these exercises and to adapt ourselves. To understand that we can pardon ourselves and develop.

That is the point at which everything changed for me. Leaving a drawn-out relationship broke me since I was unable to comprehend harming somebody near me. Somebody I genuinely thought about. Be that as it may, I needed to organize myself, my necessities, and my future. Aim matters. What's more, when your aims are in the correct spot, you will consistently discover what's intended for you and bloom.

In understanding my mankind and tolerating its defects, I discovered freedom. I discovered pardoning. I discovered mending. What's more, it put me on the way to more profound edification.

In this way, I trust every one of you excuse yourselves for whatever you've done. It's an ideal opportunity to lift the loads and to walk unreservedly. To grasp the sun and the singing feathered creatures. To appreciate the grinning faces and the glow around you. Since your slip-ups don't make you any to a lesser extent an individual. They make you human.

CHAPTER FORTY-NINE

In many cases, we permit agony and distress to change our choices. To fill us with lament. To drive us to scrutinize our decisions and our course.

In any case, we should recall why we settled on our choices. Why we left. Why we disavowed. Why we changed professions. We settled on these choices since we saw more promising times to come in them. They are simply the vehicles we have to give better. To develop and to achieve genuine bliss.

What's more, we shouldn't overlook these reasons as we're pursuing greatness and attempting to assemble ourselves. Regardless of how hard it gets. Regardless of how broken we feel.

Recollect that inward voice that was calling to you. That internal flash of expectation. Summon it now, and proceed with this way. It gets more diligently before it shows signs of improvement. You will think back on the great occasions. That is ordinary. We generally miss what's natural. Yet at the same time, commonality offers restricted development.

Also, it is your obligation to keep developing and advancing, with the goal that you may fashion the life and satisfaction you merit. It harms now, yet you will grin and be appreciative later.

CHAPTER FIFTY

I generally accepted that I needed to altruism to get love. That I needed to desert my requirements, my musings, and my sentiments. I was constantly startled by opening up and permitting my most profound articulations to rise.

I ended up dreading surrender so a lot, that I'd at last wind up relinquishing myself. What's more, others would forsake me in light of the fact that the concealment of one's most profound self represses our capacity to associate legitimately with others. It is our blemishes and our flaws that quandary us to each other. We're ready to see that we're not the only one and that we're all battling comparatively.

Be that as it may, I didn't understand this until late. Also, a ton of it had to do with my adolescence. I generally felt like a weight. Like I never really had a place. I didn't have numerous sheltered spaces in my initial a very long time to communicate and to see that my emotions and my needs would be approved.

I was molded to accept that my value was exclusively dependent upon my capacity to help other people. I was enmeshed and never figured out how to define limits. Nor was I shown the criticalness of my own needs and emotions.

However, that has changed in the wake of diving profoundly into my past and mending a great deal of it. I've discovered that adoration will never require selflessness—that is codependency. That is self-surrender. Love will consistently hold a protected space for us, particularly for our darkest minutes and our darkest parts.

Also, I need every one of you to understand that. You may think you have to altruism for adoration. In any case, that is your youth injury talking. You don't. All you requirement for genuine love is validness, trustworthiness, and weakness. Permit individuals to interface with the genuine you. Since the genuine you are commendable, and the genuine you merit authentic love.

CHAPTER FIFTY-ONE

We as a whole stick to trust. Fuel the smallest fire in our souls. Tuning in to the faintest murmurs of our still, small voice. We make some hard memories saying goodbye since we felt so profoundly. We truly had confidence in what we were building, and how we felt about someone else.

Be that as it may, we should make a qualification among the real world and dream. Do we have trust since we've seen clear signs, or do we have trust as a psyche method for dealing with stress to numb our torment? That is essential to address.

The brutal truth is that numerous individuals won't return. They will progress forward and just respect us in their recollections. Sifting through the caring occasions and the most joyful minutes. Furthermore, that is alright. That is a piece of life.

In any case, note that individuals don't remain away in light of the fact that we're "disgraceful" or "unlovable." The reasons rise above us, regularly relating to their own inward injuries and injuries.

What's more, we've all been there. We've all left, not on account of another, but since we expected to get ourselves. Recall that when somebody leaves your life.

They may return. They may not. Be that as it may, you should proceed with your excursion. You should drive yourself. You should live. There is still a ton to encounter and to appreciate. What's more, you will keep on sprouting. To rise. To become all that you're intended to be. Furthermore, it'll be your agony driving the way.

CHAPTER FIFTY-TWO

We have a feeling that we should have everything made sense of and sorted out. I realize I did. I misjudged naiveté and vulnerability for disappointment. Felt that on the off chance that I was uncertain, I will undoubtedly break my fantasies and remain ensnared in old cycles.

Be that as it may, nobody has everything made sense of. The world is awfully immense, and excessively unusual, for us to know it all. We can't be specialists. We must be human. With the entirety of our defects, our frailties, and our vulnerabilities.

However the more we live, the more we reveal. Also, that is the excellence of the obscure: we never know exactly how amazing our lives can turn out, in the event that we confide simultaneously, we accomplish the work, and we permit ourselves to develop.

Relinquish the requirement for control. Of the should be completely mindful and knowing. It'll never occur. Rather, apportion your vitality toward turning into the best form of yourself, and moving toward life as it comes. That is the manner by which we make satisfaction, and how we grasp life naturally.

I don't have everything made sense of. What's more, I never will. I'm totally surrendered to that reality. It doesn't alarm me like it used to. It empowers me to invite my humankind and to succeed normally. No limitations. No confinements. No feelings of trepidation. Just development, lowliness, and joy.

Thus, in case you're feeling lost, it's typical. We as a whole experience it. Ordinarily. However, we generally discover our direction, and we become who we're intended to be. .We have an inclination that we should have everything made sense of and composed. I realize I did. I misconstrued inability and vulnerability for disappointment. Felt that on the off chance that I was uncertain, I will undoubtedly break my fantasies and remain ensnared in old cycles.

Be that as it may, nobody has everything made sense of. The world is very immense, and excessively capricious, for us to know it all. We can't be specialists. We must be human. With the entirety of our blemishes, our frailties, and our vulnerabilities.

However the more we live, the more we reveal. What's more, that is the magnificence of the obscure: we never know exactly how excellent our lives can turn out, on the off chance that we confide all the while, we accomplish the work, and we permit ourselves to develop.

Relinquish the requirement for control. Of the should be completely mindful and knowing. It'll never occur. Rather, designate your vitality toward turning into the best form of yourself, and moving toward life as it comes. That is the manner by which we make bliss, and how we grasp life naturally.

I don't have everything made sense of. What's more, I never will. I'm totally surrendered to that reality. It doesn't surprise me like it used to. It empowers me to invite my humankind and to flourish normally. No limitations. No constraints. No feelings of dread. Just development, quietude, and bliss.

Along these lines, in case you're feeling lost, it's ordinary. We as a whole experience it. Commonly. In any case, we generally discover our direction, and we become who we're intended to be.

CHAPTER FIFTY-THREE

You will never mend through disgrace. Nor will you blossom underneath blame. You need to relinquish both blame and disgrace to push ahead. To develop. To mend and to acknowledge your humankind.

Blame and disgrace keep us in negative, redundant cycles. Since as opposed to concentrating on arrangements, we center around the mix-ups. That is no real way to push ahead.

What's more, all things considered, we as whole commit errors. We've all "remained excessively long", or picked an inappropriate individual. In any case, it's never as uneven as we might suspect. We didn't settle on specific choices since we're "inept." We made them since we put stock in them. We saw the characteristics and perspectives that gave us trust. Furthermore, it's excellent that we see the positive qualities of things.

But on the other hand, it's an ideal opportunity to begin seeing the positive qualities in ourselves. To begin grasping the adoration, the sympathy, and the quality we have. We have our wrecked hearts since we were sufficiently able to see the great and to put stock in it. Also, that is the thing that makes us uncommon. That is the thing that gives us how lovely our hearts are. There is no disgrace in that.

Along these lines, let go of your blame and your disgrace. Pardon yourself. Recognize your great characteristics. What's more, push ahead. All slip-ups are adequate. They move us to advance and reinforce us. We need them to develop and to turn into.

CHAPTER FIFTY-FOUR

We as a whole have issues. We as a whole have developed to achieve and change to make. In any case, we're not liable for others' issues, the manner in which our instabilities cause us to accept.

While love draws out the best in individuals, it additionally draws out the most exceedingly terrible. It reveals our injuries, our weaknesses, and the entirety of our smothered, unfortunate subliminal affiliations.

Also, I get this. I had the propensity for pushing kind, adoring individuals away. Right off the bat, I was persuaded that others were the issue and that I was feeling "off" in light of the fact that they simply "weren't the one." Yet as I ventured into my 20s, and experienced rehashed patterns of self-damage, I understood I had some internal injuries to recuperate.

Also, others will do likewise to you. They will drive you away when you love them right, in light of the fact that their injuries will make them accept they're disgraceful, or that something is "off," on the grounds that it's a deviation from the brokenness they've been exposed to.

In any case, that is not your issue. Your obligation is to be the best form you can and to let life follow through to its logical end. On the off chance that others can't acknowledge it, and they drive you away, that is on them. You are as yet commendable, and your affection is a blessing that recuperates.

Trust that your affection is correct and that you have shown up perfectly. That is the thing that characterizes your value. Another's the powerlessness to acknowledge a sound love is on them. You should acknowledge that and let everything go. They have their own mending to do. Furthermore, you have more love to give.

CHAPTER FIFTY-FIVE

None of us like to feel pain. It's easier to avoid. To blast music. To binge-watch a show. To hang out with friends and kick our thoughts to the side.

But eventually, we must feel it. Because it will force its way out of whatever cell we've locked it in. It will barge through our mental rooms and shout until we acknowledge it. And the longer we wait, the harder it can be.

Yet pain offers us varying perspectives—one of which is the examination of our depth and our emotionality. If you're feeling pain, it's because you opened yourself. You embraced something worthwhile. You gave your heart the free reign to feel.

And that is beautiful. That shows you your humaneness. How deep you can go and how open your soul is. Go inward. Learn from this pain. Learn from your struggles. Your heartache. Allow them all to change you for the better.

There is a lot to learn from every struggle. Suppression won't solve it. But an honest introspection will. You can do it.

CHAPTER FIFTY-SIX

Do what you feel is ideal. Remain. Leave. Express your emotions. Seek after something new. Furthermore, trust a certain something: what is intended for you, will discover you. Regardless of how far you wander. Regardless of how broken you feel.

Furthermore, it will contact you at the correct time. Since timing is everything. Timing brings out development, our change, and our advancement. We have to follow what we feel is ideal. That is the means by which we start to acknowledge who we really are, and what we need from life.

In any case, a considerable lot of us dread change and flight. We figure we might be "destroying" what's genuinely implied for us. In any case, that is bogus. Our fortunes are still in transit, anticipating us to arrive at the ideal goal.

In this way, continue onward. Settle on your decisions. Follow your heart. Jumble up. Do what you feel is ideal. What is in the most profound arrangement with your soul. And afterward, believe that it'll all work out. That you're on the correct way, and that you will get what you're chasing.

Since I'll see you. Regardless of whether you in all honesty.

CHAPTER FIFTY-SEVEN

The correct choice is the hardest to make. It will make you extremely upset. Break your reality. The power for you to reconsider your past and yourself.

In any case, it will likewise be the beginning of an extraordinary excursion. To a journey past what you've been educated, and into your own internal realities. Into the profundities that portray what your identity is, in the entirety of your rushes of significance. In the entirety of your bits of affection.

What's more, I took in this last year, when I truly began to seek after myself. At the point when I put myself first and said that my bliss matters the same amount of as anybody else's—an acknowledgment I despite everything need to reaffirm. Since when you've carried on with your life accepting that you should altruism for adoration, it's difficult to change. Difficult to accept something else. .

However, I made strides. I escaped an awful workplace. I left a four-year relationship. Separated me from individuals who were veering off than me. It hurt. My heart broke, on many occasions. Yet, I wouldn't transform anything.

Now, I'm cheerful. I'm living for me. I've found my value, in manners I never would have. What's more, you can, as well!

CHAPTER FIFTY-EIGHT

Leaving is unbearable. I despise everything recollect how crushed I was as I turned the last page of my four-year relationship. As I shut the book and threw it on the rack.

We had gone through years composing it. A long time producing recollections and showing each other more ourselves, and love. We saw noteworthy changes. We started to get ready for the future.

In any case, a quiet voice murmured disagree. What's more, I was unable to get why, with a stunning lady, and an apparently extraordinary circumstance, I was unable to settle in. It'd be simply the beginning of a profound excursion into myself. A careful assessment of my past, my childhood, and many smothered injuries. However, it wouldn't begin until I left.

What's more, a piece of me kicked the bucket that last night. Tears gushed down my face. My chest shook wildly. I felt like a sad kid who had been yanked away from his home and had to move and restart his life. I didn't realize which pieces to remake. Which twisted to join first.

In any case, presently, I understood that, however it hurt, I expected to do it. Since hurt can't redirect us based on what is essential. Torment can't occupy us. We should press forward, in the event that we realize that we're being called to another bearing. We should acknowledge the greeting and permit our more established parts to kick the bucket. They will fill in as the prolific field to plant freshness in. At that point, we can procure an ample gather.

Indeed, even I despite everything think back and reflect. Be that as it may, I'm comforted in realizing that I respected my spirit and followed my excursion. That I developed and advanced, as I was intended to. You can do likewise.

CHAPTER FIFTY-NINE

The hardest piece of proceeding onward is relinquishing the rapture and bliss we felt with another.

Up until that point, they were the best we had. The person who stirred emotions in us we esteemed dead. The person who appeared to fit all that we were searching for.

It's entirely expected to grieve the misfortune. To consider the incredible occasions. In any case, we should abstain from stalling out in resignation. Accepting that our lives will be damned and that we'll never adore again.

Since we will. Furthermore, with the exercises, we learn, and the manner in which we develop, we will accomplish an adoration that suits our higher selves. An affection that celebrates in our inward profundities and urges us to unfurl magnificently.

In this way, lament. Feel it. Let the agony meander through your body. Feel all the messed up hearts. In any case, remember that you can mend, and you will cherish once more. What's more, this time, it'll be better. You'll have a superior thought of what you need, and of what your identity is, and it'll help you on your journey.

CHAPTER SIXTY

Once in a while, we permit our agony to direct our previous accounts and our mending. We become so fascinated in our hurt, that we miss all the silver linings. All the development and the integrity we achieved.

It's anything but difficult to think back and state that we should, or shouldn't have, accomplished something. Perhaps we ought to have left sooner. Possibly we ought to have battled somewhat harder. Perhaps we ought to have communicated more. Possibly we ought to have been firmer in our limits and our facts. .

Be that as it may, we took in every exercise from the entirety of our encounters. Encounters that fill in as our present establishment. What's more, there is nothing of the sort as "an inappropriate individual." They were the opportune individual around then. The exercise you required. The way for more profound development. The token of your value and of what you may need to chip away at.

What's more, regardless of whether they're a major part of your life, it doesn't refute the exercises you've learned. Nor does it change all the integrity you can gather from the circumstance with a changed point of view.

The decision is yours. You can decide to flounder in lament, pity, and torment. Or on the other hand you can reevaluate your points of view, dispell old stories, and work to change. You aren't answerable for the agony others have caused.

Be that as it may, you are answerable for what you do with your agony and sorrow. For the manner in which you reconstruct and rise. What's more, I trust you decide to see the decency. That you grasp the exercises and the development. Since you're deserving of mending and of building a more joyful future. Be that as it may, you should focus on the work first.

CHAPTER SIXTY-ONE

Love isn't simply over the revelation of another. Love is additionally about the disclosure of ourselves. The acknowledge of who we really are, and exactly how far we're willing to go.

Love is the main device sufficiently amazing to unearth profound inside our souls to reveal all the injuries and the injuries we've covered. Love allows us to see our internal identities totally uncovered. It breaks our exteriors. Permits reality to strike us the hardest. Since we can't lie. We can't stow away. We should confront whatever it toils up.

A considerable lot of us become so focused on our affections for another, that we disregard the most basic part: the investigation of one's self. The opportunity to genuinely, and profoundly, become more acquainted with our deepest musings and sentiments.

What's more, that is the most excellent part. Since at last, you're all you have. You are the one individual who won't ever leave your own side. That is the reason it's essential to utilize love to increase further understanding into ourselves and to develop more spaces for acknowledgment, recuperating, and advancement.

In this way, if love makes them hurt or feeling contrary, that is alright. It's just highlighting some work you despite everything need to do. Try not to be embarrassed. We as a whole have it. Furthermore, we're all becoming together.

Your affection will consistently show you your own internal excellence and profundity. Furthermore, nothing outperforms that. Nothing will take you further.

CHAPTER SIXTY-TWO

Now and again, we permit our torment to direct our previous accounts and our mending. We become so charmed in our hurt, that we miss all the silver linings. All the development and the decency we accomplished.

It's anything but difficult to think back and state that we should, or shouldn't have, accomplished something. Perhaps we ought to have left sooner. Possibly we ought to have battled somewhat harder. Possibly we ought to have communicated more. Possibly we ought to have been firmer in our limits and our facts.

In any case, we took in every exercise from the entirety of our encounters. Encounters that fill in as our present establishment. What's more, there is nothing of the sort as "an inappropriate individual." They were the correct individual around then. The exercise you required. The way for more profound development. The token of your value and of what you may need to chip away at.

Furthermore, regardless of whether they're a major part of your life, it doesn't refute the exercises you've learned. Nor does it change all the decency you can gather from the circumstance with a changed point of view.

The decision is yours. You can decide to flounder in lament, pity, and agony. Or on the other hand, you can reevaluate your viewpoints, dispel old accounts, and work to change. You aren't liable for the torment others to have caused.

However, you are answerable for what you do with your torment and sorrow. For the manner in which you modify and rise. Furthermore, I trust you decide to see integrity. That you grasp the exercises and the development. Since you're deserving of recuperating and of building a more joyful future. In any case, you should focus on the work first. .

CHAPTER SIXTY-THREE

What we endure and pick says everything regarding what we accept we're deserving of. Along these lines, in case you're reliably picking, and enduring, other people who can't adore you ethically, you need to dig into yourself and reveal why. Since we're answerable for what we endure and permit.

Also, I'm not saying this to disgrace anybody. I'm stating this to move every one of us from a space of weakened victimhood to a space of engaged life and information.

It's anything but difficult to point fingers at others. To remain in the job of the person in question and to grumble concerning why we're continually dismissed and neglected. Yet, in case we're the shared factor in the condition, we should recognize that and get further.

In case you're simply the person who consistently finds wanting more and enduring abuse or others' failure to respond, at that point, it's an ideal opportunity to reveal why you're content. Why you're ready to suffer tunelessly.

Since you merit better. In any case, you'll never get it on the off chance that you don't trust it, or on the off chance that you unendingly remain in the spaces of pathetic love and unremarkable treatment. You'll never accept you're worth more on the off chance that you don't stand firm to request it and seek after it.

You are worth more than the solitary love. The grief. The failure of others to pick you. Also, you'll at long last understand that when you leave and recover your value by offering yourself to the individuals who coordinate your endeavors.

CHAPTER SIXTY-FOUR

We've been customized to accept that affection is contingent. That we should bend ourselves to get acknowledgment and warmth. That we aren't sufficient similarly as we seem to be. Along these lines, we attempt to expand ourselves. Misrepresent our characteristics and qualities. Conceal who we genuinely are.

And afterward, we wonder why we can't truly, and profoundly, interface with another. A phony piece will never finish a riddle. Also, a phony form of yourself will never finish love.

Be that as it may, we've been adapted to accept so for different reasons, for example, old-style molding in adolescence. In the event that we were "acceptable", we got parental acknowledgment, consolation, and love. However, in the event that we were "terrible", we were disgraced and rebuffed.

We convey these affiliations, and numerous different injuries, into our adulthood. Into our undertakings.

However, actually all individuals are inalienably commendable and meriting love. Without a doubt, we may need to develop and change for our own advantage, yet that doesn't imply that we're any less adorable. That we should be disgraced and restricted to forlornness.

You are sufficient. You have incredible characteristics. You are much all the more captivating on the grounds that you're despite everything developing and advancing. Since you're ready to look for, even all through such internal tempests. What's more, love acknowledges all that you are. It doesn't constrain you to be more. It might motivate you to change and develop, yet it will never drive. It will never disgrace. What's more, I trust you understand that you're deserving of it. That you will be, you have consistently been, and you will consistently be, sufficient.

CHAPTER SIXTY-FIVE

Nobody likes torment. Nobody likes falling flat. Thinking about what they fouled up and why they're contemptible. Be that as it may, there are openings in each farewell. Chances in each disappointment.

We can learn. We can increase extraordinary development. We can drive ourselves to battle more diligently for what we need.

What's more, honestly, it took me some time to understand this. So often, I needed something to work out. An occupation. A relationship. A business opportunity. What's more, in the event that it fizzled, I'd shut down and distrust that there was any possible acceptable. I caught myself in pessimism and accepted that I was bound for disappointment.

In any case, presently, I understand that I was so fortunate to encounter each disaster, disappointment, and adversity. Everything added to who I've become. Also, it's been an excellent excursion of development.

However, I could never have been pushed to develop and to prosper, in the event that I hadn't acknowledged my torment. On the off chance that I hadn't made harmony.

Also, I need every one of you to do likewise. There are many silver linings anticipating your revelation. In any case, you should open your psyche and your eyes. You should have confidence in the conceivable outcomes.

Your messed up heart, your botched chance, and your agony are largely instructing you. They're pervading you with a feeling of affection and assurance. What's more, that is the way you will rise.

CHAPTER SIXTY-SIX

I recognize what it resembles to hurt. To feel alone and deserted. To ponder when the torment and internal torture will end. To feel like not many can relate and comprehend the disarray and the hurting inside.

In any case, these dim minutes are regularly the antecedents to a colossal change. They're the entryways that welcome us into the most profound profundities of our being with the goal that we can at last start diving profoundly into ourselves and investigating what our identity is.

Agony doesn't need to be negative. It tends to be aware of go inside and to perceive what our most unhealed parts are attempting to let us know. This is the place we realize what we're missing, and how we can satisfy ourselves. How we can rise and vanquish our injuries.

Feeling lost and sad can be a decent marker that you're starting to deconstruct bogus accounts and that you're at last arousing to your internal voice and finding how you can address your issues.

All things considered, the excursion is long. The way can be deceptive and horrendous. Being separated from everyone else and confronting yourself will test you. In any case, it'll likewise fortify you. It'll show you your inward enormity and strength. Establish the framework for you to expand upon.

In this way, in case you're feeling alone, hold tight. It's not unexpected to be befuddled and to be apprehensive. In any case, you will get past this. What's more, you're going to see that you've generally had a mind-boggling measure of solidarity. That you've generally had the option to appear for yourself. Also, you required the correct minutes to delineate that.

CHAPTER SIXTY-SEVEN

Experiencing passionate feelings forgave me that adoration is unqualified. That adoration opens us and constrains us to see past "imperfections" and contrasts. That we can't control how profoundly we feel. What's more, that we will show up wonderfully and be there for somebody constantly.

Unlimited love implies that we completely acknowledge another and that we focus on supporting their development perpetually. That we will not squander a second to be there for them and to shower them with acclaim, with reverence, and with support.

What's more, on the off chance that you've adored somebody unequivocally, they were fortunate to have you. You've given them a genuine blessing. Given them what love genuinely is and how it ought to be ordered. You've given them a long-lasting plan and standard to follow.

Also, you merit the equivalent. You have the right to have somebody respond to your genuine love. Not expect you to be "more." Not reveal to you that no doubt about it or that you should be "more intelligent" "more entertaining" or "more shrewd." In light of the fact that when an association is valid, the guidelines and the necessities vacate the premises. We disregard unmistakably more than we suspected we could. .

Also, it's lovely. A solid association is a solid association. It vanquishes all. It revises the content and shows what a certifiable bond does.

At last, genuine love is sheltered. It's empowering. It's warm. Open. Understanding. It holds a space of incorporation, backing, and commitment. At that point, it permits the characteristic to unfurl. It permits two people to share, to get profound, and to develop. However, it never powers somebody to be something they're most certainly not.

CHAPTER SIXTY-EIGHT

Recuperating isn't the deletion of our sentiments. Since emotions never disappear. What's more, the more you battle them, the more you'll affix yourself to the past.

You need to recognize reality. You're harming. You're battling. You're getting pieces and battling to be entirety. Also, that is all alright. This is a piece of the procedure.

However, comprehend a certain something: endings occur for reasons. What's more, regardless of whether we concur or differ with these reasons, we can't deny their reality. We need to transparently, and unbiasedly, reflect.

What's more, this reflection can't simply concentrate on the other person. We should likewise concentrate on ourselves and review how we appeared and exactly what form of ourselves we introduced all through that time.

At that point, we need to help ourselves to remember these reasons. Furthermore, we need to recollect that we merit more than a catastrophe. More than void guarantees. More than empty words and modest forms of sentiment.

In conclusion, we need to acknowledge obligation, both for how we appear and for what we endure. We aren't casualties. In case we're showing up ineffectively, we can change. Or then again in case, we're being abused, we can request more. We are ground-breaking.

Recall why something finished. What's more, recall why you left. It's not unexpected to be harmed and contrite. Yet, there is a more promising time to come anticipating you.

CHAPTER SIXTY-NINE

At the point when you've carried on with a daily existence predicated around satisfying others, picking yourself, and battling for your own joy, will feel off-base and unnatural.

What's more, when numerous individuals feel off and agitated, they consequently assume they've settled on an inappropriate choice and they run back to what's natural—regardless of whether it harms them and keeps them abandoned.

I know this well. I was so used to relinquishing my wants to appease others. In this way, when I at long last began picking myself, saying "no," and leaving whatever neglected to profit me, I felt irregular. Truth be told, I nearly felt wiped out.

Be that as it may, those sentiments of repugnance are the door to change. They're the last level we should finish to get our new refined selves. It won't be anything but difficult to bring an end to these propensities. It will take a ton and it will deplete you now and again.

Keep in mind: you will battle to change. You're revamping old propensities and old examples that you've had for a considerable length of time. It'll take some time.

Be that as it may, I need you to recall this: your bliss is far more prominent than all else. What's more, you should pick yourself. You should respect your wants, with the goal that you reaffirm a basic message: you matter. Your requirements and your sentiments are similarly as significant as somebody else's.

Furthermore, on the off chance that you need to leave a poisonous relationship, an unfortunate relational intricacy, and a hopeless occupation to pick up your joy, you should. You have the right to. Regardless of whether you feel unnatural, you're settling on the correct decisions. You're picking yourself. That is not off-base.

CHAPTER SEVENTY

With regard to cherish, I don't know a lot. What's more, believe it or not, very few of us do—despite the fact that we like to believe we're specialists.

However, there's one thing I know: when you truly love somebody, and you genuinely observe their spirit completely, you won't care about the standards, the specifications, and the rules you were educated. You will be constrained to break the shows and to go burst through the entryways of their heart uproariously.

You will start to see that affection, my companions, is an assortment of things. Furthermore, maybe the best portrayal is mysteriously mystical. We're attracted to another. We feel a massive association. We share things and have our weaknesses tried. We feel profound and we come to know portions of ourselves we've since a long time ago stifled.

What's more, we understand something: love is best given when an acknowledgment is behind it. At the point when we understand that we don't should be something so huge for somebody to cherish us. We should simply act naturally. Show our certainties. Talk transparently. Live submissively and genuinely.

However numerous individuals miss this since they're acclimated with adoration being restrictive and dependent upon their conduct. Be that as it may, I guarantee you: when you're really cherished for what your identity is, you will be sufficient. Your imperfections won't make any difference so much. Your injuries won't be terrible. Everything will be acknowledged as the work of art that you may be, and you will sparkle since you're being cherished right.

CHAPTER SEVENTY-ONE

Numerous individuals believe that they recuperate when they quit cherishing somebody and delete every one of their sentiments. Be that as it may, that is suppression. That is denying reality and further harming yourself.

You don't quit cherishing somebody. Nor will you totally annihilate all recollections. You'll generally muse on specific occasions. Continuously wonder what could have happened in an unexpected way. That is the profundity of your own affection.

Furthermore, however it harms, it doesn't require the disgracing of affection. It's not loving that harms us. It's our concept of it. It's the individuals we pursue who will in general injury us and stir our frailties.

Be that as it may, that is alright. That is the reason endings are helpful: they permit us to see these examples and these facts, and afterward, we can work to recuperate. We can work to change.

Acknowledge your emotions. Acknowledge that you love somebody and that it's thoroughly fine to even now consider the past and to ponder. You won't remain there until the end of time. In any case, you will trap yourself in the event that you deny your sentiments. Grasp everything, and afterward work to change.

CHAPTER SEVENTY-TWO

Excusing myself was an immense battle. I was in every case excessively basic. Put me in the spotlight and disgraced me for past slip-ups. Offended me and executed severe rules to guarantee I wouldn't destroy once more.

Be that as it may, these undesirable measures were counterproductive. I'd even now commit errors—and that is on the grounds that I'm human. I'm error-prone. We as a whole are. We're going to waver and slip. We're going to hurt others and take negative ways.

What's more, I discovered that when I left. I was unable to acknowledge the way that I left a four-year relationship. I castigated myself for harming another and accepted that I didn't merit satisfaction as a result of it. Along these lines, I'd unendingly think I was contemptible and I'd unwittingly damage the decency that was coming to my direction. Be that as it may, I changed.

Also, I'm happy I did. We're all going to commit errors and jumble up. It's a piece of the ride. All things considered, we're deserving of our own empathy and pardoning. We don't have to kill ourselves for botches. We can move toward them inquisitively, try to comprehend, and afterward tenderly work to change them.

Along these lines, let it go. It doesn't make a difference in what you did. What you said. How you fizzled. You're human. It's the manner by which you rise and how you develop that matters. What's more, insofar as you're attempting, you don't have anything to lament.

CHAPTER SEVENTY-THREE

Awfulness and torment offer you a brilliant, uncommon chance to reconsider yourself and your activities. They offer you an opportunity to gain proficiency with your value.

Since here's a mystery: in case you're continually getting your heartbroken, you don't have the foggiest idea about your value—and I'm not saying this to stigmatize you. In any case, consider it: on the off chance that you truly knew your value, and saw your boundless excellence in your extraordinary characteristics, you wouldn't invest so much energy pursuing others for approval. You wouldn't detain yourself in circumstances where self-deserting is ensured.

We will in general romanticize others as we deny, and disregard, ourselves. Be that as it may, in the event that we began to really laud ourselves and spotlight on our extraordinary characteristics, the manner in which we accomplish for a sentimental accomplice and others, we'd see a huge improvement.

What's more, tragedy offers this chance. Tragedy allows us to look at each messed up pieces and to fix it with adoration. With empathy. With an unanticipated, however genuinely necessary, receptiveness.

Better believe it, it harms. You're learning your value. You're pulverizing old establishments. You're obliterating old examples. It will get appalling. Yet, you will gain proficiency with your value. And afterward, you will become who want and you're going to produce the best life and love.

CHAPTER SEVENTY-FOUR

At the point when we lose something incredible, we trust it's the end. We accept that we're never going to adore again and that we're bound for unceasing grief. For agonizing despondency. Desolate, throbbing evenings.

What's more, I comprehend. Endings are hard. They devastate our present real factors and power us to modify them. They open the entirety of our concealed agonies and injuries. They make us face ourselves—and that is the hardest part. Since we've all been attempting to keep away from that, either intentionally or subliminally.

All things considered, we can mend. We can reproduce and reclassify ourselves with the messed up pieces and the new exercises we've achieved. What's more, here's another reality: possibly you won't remember a similar love. I'd really ensure that you won't.

Be that as it may, you'll experience a superior love and an additionally satisfying relationship since you'll have another, refined establishment to put together it with respect to. An establishment developed with a more profound comprehension of your internal identity, your preferences, your aversions, and your wants.

Shock constrains us to rethink ourselves and to redo obsolete convictions. That is a gift. That is the thing that we require for change. What's more, that is the means by which we gain the profound, sweeping affection we're chasing.

CHAPTER SEVENTY-FIVE

So often, our feelings of dread—and not our activities—are the very things that limit our capacity to inundate ourselves in adoration. Our feelings of dread keep us from being open and from indicating our most profound profundities. The very profundities that others can associate with.

We're unnerved of demonstrating these profundities on the grounds that in past connections, or in youth, they were dismissed. We disguised this dismissal as close to home incompetence and swore subliminal promises to never show them again.

One more's dismissal of us really will in general be a dismissal of themselves. Individuals reject the parts in you that compel them to go up against themselves. It's not about you.

In any case, I'll mention to you what is about you. Your dread. Your trepidation. Your powerlessness to relinquish old accounts and old hurt. These issues are tormenting you and obstructing your capacity to increase a healthy love.

I was a survivor of this. I was consistently hesitant to share. Continuously apprehensive that if individuals saw my "blemishes" and my unhealed parts, they'd lose love for me and surrender me.

I wasn't right. I've since seen that it is my uncovered altruism and my exposed crudeness that permits others to give themselves all the more transparently, in this manner holding us more profound together. Your defects occupy the space with straightforwardness and love.

Also, you ought to be powerless and show your haziest, most unhealed parts to the individuals who love you. That is the manner by which you'll go further, and how you'll accomplish bona fide love. Do we risk getting injured? Sure. Be that as it may, it's smarter to cherish and to encounter, than to carry on with our lives in vacancy sustained by harmful stories and misshaped accounts. Love will consistently leave endowments that void can never leave.

CHAPTER SEVENTY-SIX

I compared the weakness to the threat. To mayhem and inconvenience. I detested being defenseless in light of the fact that I felt that it would enable others to abuse me.

Furthermore, I saw that, in addition to the fact that I struggled to be open to other people, yet in addition to myself. I detested going up against my feelings. Despised feeling like I was suffocating each time I'd ponder something. Along these lines, I'd curb my emotions. Lock my feelings into a psychological basement and decline to recognize them.

This was never more harmful to me than a year ago. So much occurred. Particularly the end of a four-year relationship. I wouldn't confront my sentiments. I was alarmed by the distress and misery. Of dealing with another reality. In any case, this suppression just exacerbated the situation.

After some time, the agony kept rotting until it'd eject indiscriminately minutes, and I'd be left shocked and perplexed, asking why, on specific days, I was fat more discouraged and drained.

Furthermore, I don't need every one of you to experience these passionate dividers. Since you will in the event that you won't face your considerations and your emotions. You should stand up to them. What's more, you should show restraint toward yourself all through the procedure. Lamenting is a long, tempestuous excursion. However, it's the way we mend. It's the manner by which we reclassify ourselves.

Thus, conscious of whatever is harming you. Permit it to ascend to the surface. Anticipate that it should hurt. Anticipate that it should be troublesome. Anticipate that it should require some investment. Furthermore, in conclusion, anticipate that you should have the option to defeat it. Since you can, and you will. Be that as it may, you should initially move toward yourself straightforwardly, truly, and energetically.

CHAPTER SEVENTY-SEVEN

Numerous individuals accept that, when their brains return to old examples, that they aren't mending. That they're destined to be stuck in anguish or undesirable examples. In any case, that is not the situation.

Mending is an excursion. It includes extraordinary days and terrible days. Snapshots of certainty and win, and snapshots of uncertainty and antagonism. You won't generally feel incredible. Nor will you have the option to break and change profoundly settled in subliminal examples right away.

It requires some investment. Your brain battles and hooks onto these implanted convictions since that has been its endurance instrument for a considerable length of time. That doesn't just disperse. You should keep accomplishing the work.

It's not unexpected to feel like no doubt about it or that your feelings are furious. Its methods for uncertain injuries and agonies are surfacing, and your psyche is acclimating to manage them. Keep practicing persistence and sympathy for yourself.

Injuries are genuine and they require coordinated exertion for goal. I'm a piece of numerous gatherings, and numerous individuals talk about the fact that it is so normal to encounter falling go into old propensities and examples. Utilize those minutes as a chance to additionally investigate yourself.

CHAPTER SEVENTY-EIGHT

Possibly you're harmed. Possibly you're grieving a noteworthy misfortune and reviling the universe for making you extremely upset. Perhaps you're lamenting the way that your affection was starcrossed.

Be that as it may, you shouldn't. Since regardless of whether it finished, and regardless of whether your heart is broken, you have great recollections. What's more, those are extremely valuable.

Life has its good and bad times. Times where we grin joyfully and feel that it couldn't be any better. At that point the occasions where our hearts throb and it damages to haul ourselves up.

What's more, you realize what energizes our spirits with trust and cuts blesses our appearances? Recollections.

Recollections are the guardians of human expectation and strength. Recollections fill in as the outline and the establishment with which we look at and we dream. Recollections are what flood our hearts at 2 AM and actuate us to pursue our desires.

We might be harmed, however, we should recollect that we're harming in light of the fact that we have lovely recollections that we're grieving. Be that as it may, they will return. The future will allow you more ardent minutes that will become recollections. Also, the cycle will proceed: your heart will lock onto them and esteem them during other dim occasions.

It's a flawlessly, distinctively human way. What's more, recollections are the means. Recollections are the aides.

We thoroughly take care of recollections. What's more, however, they may involve anguish, distress, and thoughtfulness, we should recollect the excellence, the exercises, and the expectation they give.

CHAPTER SEVENTY-NINE

We as a whole accept that our affection can change another. That out of nowhere, and phenomenally, it will captivate them and spur them to be somebody, and something, they're most certainly not. We give and we give. We pour each ounce of our affection into broken hearts and relationally repressed individuals knowing, full well, that no one but they can get themselves straightened out.

And afterward, we are resentful at them for neglecting to appear for us. We can hardly imagine how our affection became lost despite a general sense of vigilance of cracked hearts and open hands, and that after, we were left with broken pieces and unanswered inquiries of our own.

In any case, here's the agonizing truth: we have to quit assuming the job of the self-important saint. The person who gives with secretive desires, trusting that somebody will respond and pick us. It's deceitful and it includes pointless weight.

Pursuing relationally stunted individuals and attempting to recuperate broken hearts are certain approaches to hurt ourselves and deny us from encountering satisfaction. We have to consider ourselves responsible. We have to pay attention to individuals' words and torments and understand that in the event that they have mending to do, it's on them. Our adoration won't speed up their recuperating.

Help yourself out by drawing your own limits. So no to passionate inaccessibility. The state no to pursuing broken hearts. Disapprove of an absence of correspondence. You can hold sympathy for harming people. However, you don't have to mend, and fix, them. You are committed to seeking after what lines up with your deepest longings. Also, if it's healthiness and unbridled love, you should pick in an unexpected way.

CHAPTER EIGHTY

Love is an incredible power. It breathes life into us. It drives us to give, to open, and to forfeit more than everything else will. .

However, in some cases, love isn't sufficient. Love doesn't accommodate the vacancy we feel from neglected requirements and negligible exertion. Love doesn't delete the scars of abuse and never-ending deserting. Love doesn't supplant exertion.

Since you can adore an individual, or an individual can cherish you, however in the event that exertion isn't underneath that affection, it'll breakdown. You will be left in the rubble of anguish and distress. .

Also, that is the reason I'm supporting for you to dig profoundly into yourself. In case you're adoring somebody and giving them your everything, you're despite everything managing ceaseless surrender and below average exertion, at that point you have to reevaluate the circumstance. .

Your value is characterized inside. Each way you appear, you love hard, you empower, and you bolster must be coordinated. That is the absolute minimum. That is the thing that you merit. Also, in case you're not getting that, it's an ideal opportunity to proceed onward. It's an ideal opportunity to cherish yourself more and to stand firm. .

Supposing that you don't battle for what you merit, you'll never get it. You'll remain ensnared in average quality. You'll rest with a developing opening in your heart. With a distressed inner voice asking you "why?" .

Cherishing somebody is excellent. Be that as it may, it's much more lovely, and all the more fulfilling, when our endeavors are responded. At the point when another person conveys their heap and appears for us. Also, you're deserving of that. You merit it. Leave the ones and the circumstances who oppose that.

CHAPTER EIGHTY-ONE

Numerous individuals accept that the cutting off of their association implies sat around. I'm certain possibly you, or somebody near you, has communicated a portion of these things:

"I went through a half year of my life to no end!" Or "I can't accept this was each of the a waste." .

Be that as it may, there is nothing of the sort as a "squander." Each relationship is an encounter. It's an open door for profound contemplation. An opportunity to perceive what you're made out of and what you may need to take a shot at. .

Since connections reflect the bond we had with our guardians, will undoubtedly show both our best, and our most noticeably awful, parts. What's more, that is the thing that we need. We mustn't fear our "defects" or wounds. We should accept each open door to investigate them, with the goal that we can keep improving.

.

There are consistently extremely valuable exercises. Exercises that guide you in the development of a superior self and a superior future. Also, I can bear witness to this. .

At the point when my four-year relationship finished, I needed to sit and reflect. I needed to at long last face my torment and quite a bit of my uncertain injuries. Also, however it crushed me, I had the option to see such a significant number of excellent exercises I gathered. I discovered that affection is sheltered. That it is conceivable to genuinely appreciate another person. However, I additionally discovered that I had a lot of recuperating to do. What's more, that was the defining moment. .

No relationship is a waste. You generally leave with something. You generally get familiar with yourself. You see that you do appear well, or that perhaps you have to some additional mending. In any case, everything adds to a superior future.

82 & To Be Continued!

Endings hurt for additional reasons than a goodbye. Certainly, we're relinquishing an individual, or a fantasy, that we had high trusts in.

Be that as it may, endings additionally uncover the entirety of our unfortunate put away subliminal affiliations relating to dismissal, deserting, weakness, and dread. We feel an inundation of feelings. What's more, we're left reeling.

However a completion is additionally the finish of your previous self. The self that continually self-yielded. That relinquished its most flawless wants and certainties. That continually attempted to fit in and acquire love.

What's more, there is nothing more enabling than understanding that old, unfortunate propensities can likewise die in a consummation, with the goal that we can reproduce ourselves and instill more beneficial ideas of self esteem, limits, trustworthiness and validness.

We don't need to rehash cycles. We can utilize the agony of a closure of look profoundly inside ourselves, and to understand what's causing this hurt and this torment, with the goal that we can adjust our choices to change the results. What's going on with everything empowered me the most.

Since I generally felt caught. Detained in a hopeless, apparently unchangeable cycle. Be that as it may, endings indicated me in an unexpected way. Endings propelled me, through agony, to dive further into myself and to at long last stand up to the entirety of my put away affiliations.

What's more, I'm happy I did. I currently am enabled to actualize important changes and to say goodbye to the accounts and the pieces of me that no longer serve my development. And every one of you can, as well.

www.ingramcontent.com/pod-product-compliance
Lightning Source LLC
Chambersburg PA
CBHW031739130726
48008CB00011BA/52

* 9 7 9 8 8 9 4 1 5 7 3 2 0 *